Waiti

Advent and Christmas
2024–2025

Jessie Bazan

LITURGICAL PRESS
Collegeville, Minnesota

litpress.org

Nihil Obstat: Rev. Robert C. Harren, J.C.L., *Censor Librorum*
Imprimatur: ✠ Most Rev. Patrick M. Neary, C.S.C., Bishop of
St. Cloud, March 20, 2024

Cover design by Monica Bokinskie.
Cover art courtesy of Getty Images.

ISSN: 1550-803X
ISBN: 978-0-8146-6717-0   978-0-8146-6719-4 (ebook)

Introduction

Stories rise like incense across the coffee shop. As I cozy up at the corner table, the insight strikes anew: everyone—and everything—in this place carries stories.

We are all story-bearers. The high schoolers giggling in the corner. The barista with their tattooed arm. The doctor with her double espresso. The Bible open in front of me. All of us bear witness to the people, places, and experiences that shape our lives. Stories of love and loss. Stories of grief and gratitude. The ordinary moments and the extraordinary ones. Sacred stories abound.

This book includes many stories from people, places, and experiences that can help us come to know the incarnate Christ more deeply. Each day of the Advent and Christmas seasons pairs a short story with a spiritual reflection, meditation, and prayer.

Women in particular inspired this book. As I prayed with the stories of Scripture, I noticed the following themes reflected in each week of lectionary readings. These themes will help us prepare our hearts for the new life that is Christ:

- Week 1 tells of *conceiving life.*
- Week 2 tells of *preparing for new life.*
- Week 3 tells of *laboring life into the world.*
- Week 4 tells of *beholding new life.*
- Week 5 tells of *beginning again with new life.*
- Week 6 tells of *journeying through life.*

I hope the stories and reflections shared in these pages will accompany and inspire you to recognize the divine presence and scriptural wisdom alive in your daily life. I also hope that our reflection on these themes will help us increase our appreciation of Christ's incarnate presence in all people.

Finally, I want to express profound gratitude to the many people whose stories form this book and who have helped me come to know God more deeply: Mom, Dad, Sam, Grandma, Grandpa, Fr. Anderson, Teresa, Lisa, Allison, Rose, David Paul, Nick, Steve, Timothy, Andrew, Mary, Katharine, Ben, Cody, Mary Ann, Bailey, Leo, Ellie, Jane, Kathleen, and the monastic communities of Saint Benedict's Monastery and Saint John's Abbey.

May the love of community overflow as together we wait in joyful hope for the coming of our Savior, Jesus Christ.

—Jessie Bazan

FIRST WEEK OF ADVENT

December 1: First Sunday of Advent

Hushed with Wonder

Readings: Jer 33:14-16; 1 Thess 3:12–4:2; Luke 21:25-28, 34-36

Scripture:
"There will be signs in the sun, the moon, and the stars . . ." (Luke 21:25)

Reflection: I press my forehead against the chilled window-sill, hushed with wonder.

Falling flakes sparkle in the streetlight. Trees barren just hours ago are now dressed in long, white gloves. The ground glistens. No prints or paws are yet crunched in the sidewalk. Everything looks crisp, clean. I breathe in the season's first snow. The glass fogs before my face. A veteran plow driver makes an initial rumble down the street. Then, the world outside my window grows quiet.

For a fleeting moment, this place—and this heart—are at peace.

———

Jesus implores his disciples to pay attention to creation. Nature will mark the coming of the Son of Man. Humankind will learn of the power of God through signs in the sun, the moon, and the stars. Redemption will be made known in the roaring seas and passing clouds.

Luke's apocalyptic scene is much less serene than the one outside my window, but the call to action remains the same: Stop. Look. Listen. Feel. Awe at the world around you.

For God created all of it, everything that lives and moves and has its being here. God loves all of it, and God promises to make every inch of this earth whole again one day.

Throughout the Advent season, we rejoice that our God chooses not to stay hidden in the heavens. Quite the opposite. God's only Son comes to dwell in *this* world. It is in *this* world that God's kingdom breaks forth. It is to *this* world that we are called to pay attention.

Meditation: Conception occurs all over the created world. Trees drop their seeds. Animals mate with one another. New patterns form across skies and seas.

Go outside and look up. Notice how the clouds dance into different forms with each passing moment. What might God be revealing to you through creation today?

Prayer: Creator God, you reflect on all you make and call it good. Foster in our communities a deeper respect for the natural world. Help us recognize the divine presence everywhere so the natural world might be met with the reverence it deserves.

December 2: Monday of the First Week of Advent

God Is Here, Too

Readings: Isa 2:1-5; Matt 8:5-11

Scripture:
[Jesus] said to him, "I will come and cure him." (Matt 8:7)

Reflection: My laptop sits on the counter in my kitchen-turned-sanctuary for another round of livestreamed liturgy. It's one of those early pandemic pivot points when the hope of *Surely this can't last more than a few weeks* loses out to the dread of *We're in this for the long haul, aren't we?* I stare at my KitchenAid covered in cookie dough and miss the smells and bells of Sunday mornings in church: incense and organs and sun streaking through stained-glass windows.

It takes me more than a few weeks of watching Mass in my pajamas to consider: *Maybe God is here, too.*

———————

A centurion alerts Jesus to the plight of his servant lying paralyzed at home. Jesus does not demand that the servant be brought to the temple. Jesus does not say healing only happens in overtly holy places. Instead, the Son of God tells the centurion, "I will come and cure him."

The Son of God says: I will come *to you.*

Jesus offers to enter under the centurion's own roof. In doing so, he reminds us that we can encounter the divine presence everywhere. Anywhere we go—or don't go—Christ is there, too. Coming together as church *in* church is a wonderful gift when it can happen safely. But God dwells in our ordinary spaces and places, too. The Son of God, the Christ child born in a barn, meets us even in the messes of ordinary life—and thankfully, he never demands that the dishes be done first.

Meditation: Conception happens amid the messes of daily life. New insights and opportunities can emerge from the ordinary if we open our senses to the possibilities.

Look around your living space with gratitude. Listen to it with intention. Notice something your eyes or ears often glaze over, like an old photograph tacked on the bulletin board or the low hum of the refrigerator. Give thanks to God for all that is—and all that could be—in this sacred space.

Prayer: Gracious God, attune our senses to your unwavering presence in our lives. Make yourself known in ordinary times and places, especially when we feel most alone.

December 3: Saint Francis Xavier

Savor the Small

Readings: Isa 11:1-10; Luke 10:21-24

Scripture:
[A]nd from his roots a bud shall blossom. (Isa 11:1)

Reflection: A once-in-a-generation storm hit Collegeville, Minnesota, on the humid evening of June 27, 1894. Heavy clouds rolled in as the sun set. An eerie calm quieted the trees.

Then the tornado touched down. Limbs snapped. Roots ripped. Branches went flying. What took seconds to level would take decades to grow anew.

But the forest would flourish again. One of the Benedictine monks who lived on the land asked his forester brothers to send seeds from their home in Germany. The seeds—red pine, Scots pine, and Norway spruce—set sail and eventually made their way into central Minnesota soil. Growth underground took time and trust. Darkness needed space to work.

Now, more than a century later, these trees stand as some of the state's oldest reforested plants. Birds nest in their branches. Animals crawl up and down their trunks. People pass under their shade.

Isn't it amazing what things so small can become?

———

A signal for the nations stems from a single shoot. A peaceful kingdom emerges in the play space of a calf, young lion, and little child. Children are chosen over the wise and learned to receive God's secrets. Once upon a time, the Son of God was little, too. Small enough to fit inside a woman's womb.

Look who he became.

We're in the midst of a season of big: big gifts to buy, big problems to solve, big storms to clean up. The magnitude of this time of year—of this time in history—can feel overwhelming. Let Advent be a season of savoring the small. Let it be a time to anticipate with great hope all that the smallest of seeds and saviors can become.

Meditation: Conception starts small. The tiniest connections can spark new life. So today, start. Simply start. Try out a new prayer practice or exercise routine. Read the first chapter of the book collecting dust on your nightstand. Start something meaningful and see where it takes you.

Prayer: God of hope, your Son entered the world through the womb of a woman. Grant us the courage to conceive small acts of kindness and bring them to fruition in our daily lives.

December 4: Wednesday of the First Week of Advent

Promised Presence

Readings: Isa 25:6-10a; Matt 15:29-37

Scripture:
Even though I walk in the dark valley
    I fear no evil; for you are at my side . . . (Ps 23:4)

Reflection: *God loves us.*

When the dreaded diagnosis comes back positive,
    God loves us.

When shame threatens to squash a fresh start,
    God loves us.

When unkind words sting an already hurting heart,
    God loves us.

When we can't muster the poise to go with grace,
    God loves us.

In those late, lonely hours fixated on what could've or
    should've been, *God loves us.*

———————

This is the season to rest assured that God loves us.
Through thick and through thin, through life and through
death, we dwell with a God whose love knows no bounds.

Because sometimes dark valleys stay dark. Sometimes
cures don't come. Sometimes crowds leave hungry. And yet

the Good Shepherd promises presence. Might this too be gift?

Advent is the time to take to heart the psalmist's testimony: "I shall live in the house of the Lord all the days of my life" (23:6). *All* the days, the psalmist declares. From dark valley days to lavish banquet days. From joyful days to miserable days. From days of triumph to days when all you want to do is crawl into bed and weep. The psalmist promises that God will remain at our sides, ready to revive our drooping spirits and welcome us into the divine home . . . *all* the days of our lives.

Meditation: Conception can be filled with unknowns. What happens now? What happens next? The start of a new reality is not always welcomed. Conceiving of next steps after the loss of a job or the death of a loved one can carry profound pain.

Check in with a neighbor or colleague who has recently experienced an unexpected loss. Offer support as they wade into a future yet unknown.

Prayer: Ever-present God, you accompany us through the ups and downs of life. Fortify our spirits that we might enter new chapters of our lives with courage.

Trust Together

Readings: Isa 26:1-6; Matt 7:21, 24-27

Scripture:
Trust in the Lord forever! (Isa 26:4)

Reflection: Malcolm probably doesn't remember me, but I think often of the morning we met—Pancake Friday at the neighborhood shelter. I was wiping down tables after the breakfast rush when I heard a voice perfect for smooth jazz radio laughing across the hall. Malcolm, a grandfatherly figure who I later learned sleeps in a storage locker most nights, sauntered over and declared: "Young lady, I know there's a God. Let me tell you why."

More than a decade out, I can't recall many details of his witness—just that forty-five minutes later, I knew there was a God, too.

———————

The command to trust gets thrown around a lot in religious circles. *If only you had more trust in the Lord. Just trust this is part of God's plan.* But what does it really take to trust God— especially in times of trial? In days of darkness? In seasons of uncertainty?

Isaiah calls the Israelites to "[t]rust in the Lord forever" after years of exile. These are hungry, hurting people. They have no interest in platitudes or cheap problem-solving. In calling for trust, Isaiah focuses not on what God will do or when God will do it. Instead, he focuses on *who God is* for the people—an eternal Rock. He draws attention to the strong, stable relationship between the Israelites and their God.

The wise prophet knows trust only happens together. Day by day, side by side, we can cultivate ever-deepening trust in our God who longs to make us whole.

Meditation: Conception invites us to trust. God calls humankind to be co-creators of this world. We do not create alone.

Reflect on your relationship with the divine. What name or image of God do you often turn to? Try praying with a different image of the divine, perhaps one used during the Advent season like *Emmanuel* or *Wonder-Counselor*.

Prayer: Eternal Rock, surround us with your beauty, sustain us with your love, and empower us with your Spirit.

Empowering the People

Readings: Isa 29:17-24; Matt 9:27-31

Scripture:
"Let it be done for you according to your faith." (Matt 9:29)

Reflection: You taught me how to throw a changeup. How to make the ball break at just the right time, control the tempo, keep the other team on their toes. You showed me the ropes of leadership: last to leave the field, first to high-five, when to dig deep, how to embrace a strength only you could see.

You were there for the first playoff win, home run, and broken heart. You did the best a coach could. Now it's my time to step up to the plate.

––––––––––

Jesus could have decided what the two blind men needed before they even had to ask. He could have saved some time and granted them sight on the spot. He's the Son of God, after all. Permission not needed to perform miracles.

But Jesus takes a different approach.

He empowers the people in front of him to be active agents in their own healing. Jesus does not assume these men want their vision restored. Not everyone without sight longs to see. Only after the men follow Jesus, approach Jesus, cry out to Jesus, and affirm their belief in Jesus' power to heal does the Son of God open their eyes.

Our God is not like a puppeteer, directing each moment of every day. Rather, God acts like a loving coach, striving to get the best out of everyone by empowering us to claim our gifts and advocate for our needs when life throws us a curve.

Meditation: Conception can be an empowering experience. God grants each of us the ability to create and grow. We learn the ropes from others who have walked similar paths.

Write a note of gratitude to a mentor who empowered you. Perhaps this is someone from earlier in life, like a high school teacher or coach. Perhaps it is your current boss or a family member who takes particular interest in your development.

Prayer: Triune God, foster healthy relationships among your people. Inspire us to accompany and empower one another as we move through life.

December 7: Saint Ambrose

Moved with Mercy

Readings: Isa 30:19-21, 23-26; Matt 9:35–10:1, 5a, 6-8

Scripture:
At the sight of the crowds, his heart was moved with pity
for them . . . (Matt 9:36)

Reflection: "You'll understand when you become parents
one day!"

A friend's comment cuts across the coffee shop like a knife
to your hearts. You long to be parents with every fiber of
your beings. For years you've tried to conceive. For years
the test strips have shown nothing but a single line.

*As if getting pregnant is easy! As if parenthood is guaranteed
for anyone who hopes hard enough!*

———

Hope.

What to do when the Advent promise feels hollow? When
hope cycles into disappointment time and time again?

The Gospels assure us that Jesus' heart responds with
mercy. Throughout his years of ministry, Jesus stayed present
to his people—close enough to see and hear and touch. Close
enough for his heart to move with mercy at their pain.

A heart does not move with mercy unless that heart under-
stands on an embodied level something of the other's pain.
Jesus knows what it's like to be judged, forgotten, cast aside.

We need look no further than his final days for proof. Ours is a God who can empathize with the troubled and abandoned because he experienced trouble and abandonment too.

Jesus' ministry was not primarily about fixing *for* but about feeling *with*. The Son of God pays attention to the lost sheep. Like a faithful shepherd, he stays alongside his sheep until each one returns safely home.

On the season's dark days, when everything is not merry and bright, let us hold tight to the truth that our God *gets it*. Our God gets *us*.

Meditation: Conception does not always happen immediately. Sometimes it does not happen at all. Too often, people end up carrying those dashed dreams alone. Holiday times can be hard for many people, particularly a holiday that celebrates the birth of a baby.

Hold individuals and couples facing infertility in intentional prayer during these sacred days.

Prayer: Merciful God, hold in your gentle care all those struggling to conceive a baby or any other dream. Make yourself known in their lives that they may feel loved and supported.

SECOND WEEK OF ADVENT

December 8: Second Sunday of Advent

In the Particulars

Readings: Bar 5:1-9; Phil 1:4-6, 8-11; Luke 3:1-6

Scripture:
In the fifteenth year of the reign of Tiberius Caesar . . .
(Luke 3:1)

Reflection: A cafeteria worker lowers boxes filled with pasta salad and beef stew into the backseat of my car. On the dashboard sits a list of names and room numbers for 29 unhoused folks staying at the hotel a few miles away. I never imagined the Eucharist could smell like beef stew until today. A litany of praise pours forth as I drive away:

> *Praise be for full back seats.*
> *Praise be for neighbors meeting neighbors.*
> *Praise be for shared dinners.*
> *Praise be for new rituals.*
> *Praise be for Eucharist in many forms.*
> *Praise be God, in this time and place.*

———————

Light of the world. King of the universe. Prince of peace. These Advent names for Jesus reflect the boundless nature of God who is above all and through all and in all. It is impossible to comprehend the vastness of God—a human limitation that can make God feel far away.

Which is why it can help at this time of year to read ancient names like "Lysanias" and "Caiaphas" and "Tiberius Caesar." To remember the high priests and rulers of first century Rome. To recall that God entered the world in and through Christ at a *particular* time in history. A time of political strife and violent uprising. A time when Pontius Pilate dictated the laws of the land, and no one seemed safe. Our boundless God lived—and died—through the turmoil of that particular time. And our God continues to show up in the particulars of here and now.

Meditation: Preparing for new life takes place in the particulars. What does preparing for the birth of Christ look like for you in this specific season of life?

Practice the *Examen* as a means of reflecting on your day. This daily prayer invites us to review the day with gratitude, naming particular emotions that arose during the day, recognizing God's presence in particular times and places, and asking for God's help tomorrow.

Prayer: God of all times and seasons, thank you for your steadfast presence among us. Continue to reveal yourself in our preparations for the days ahead.

Let the Impossible Become Possible

Readings: Gen 3:9-15, 20; Eph 1:3-6, 11-12; Luke 1:26-38

Scripture:
"[F]or nothing will be impossible for God." (Luke 1:37)

Reflection: "No, Jessie. This way!"

I look up at my friend's son with a puzzled eye. He has enlisted my help in assembling a few hundred wooden tracks in his playroom-turned-train-station. Apparently, he sees an issue with my handiwork.

"But this is how the tracks are supposed to go," I counter. As if *should* matters more than *could*. As if playing by the rules ever changed the world.

"But what about the bridge?!" he asks.

This set didn't come with a bridge, I think, until he slides a neon block from another game under a section of tracks and beams: "Now it's ready!"

For the next few minutes until snack time, his train glides over the track and flies over the bridge—almost like it was made to do just that.

———

An angel visits a poor country girl. Tells her she's full of grace. Tells her she will bear God's Son. Uses words like "great" and "holy" about the miracle in her womb. Of course she wonders: *How can this be? How does a virgin get pregnant? What does the strangest of futures have in store?* The angel gives no concrete answers. No directions or plan. Just the assurance that God can make anything happen, the promise that the Lord will be with her every step of the way.

This is enough for the poor country girl.

She believes.

She consents.

She says yes: *Let the impossible become possible within me.*

Meditation: Preparing for new life can spark creativity. Where is your energy flowing as you stand on the cusp of change? Where does your imagination long to run?

Do something today that stimulates your creativity. Try a new recipe. Pull out watercolors. Listen to inspiring music. Allow yourself to get caught up in the possibilities that await.

Prayer: God of all wisdom, you created Mary free from sin and gave her the courage to say yes to birthing your Son into the world. Grace us with the faithfulness to follow your creative promptings in our lives.

Wildness and Wonder

Readings: Isa 40:1-11; Matt 18:12-14

Scripture:
In the desert prepare the way of the LORD! (Isa 40:3)

Reflection: Hasidic Jews tell the tale of a rabbi's son who became fond of roaming the woods. His father grew worried. Who knew what predators prowled around the bend? In time he asked his son, "Why is it that you go walking in the woods each day?"

The boy replied, "I go to the woods to find God."

"How wonderful that you are searching for God," assured the father. "But, my son, you need not go anywhere special to meet the Holy One. God is the same everywhere."

"That's true," the boy answered. "But I'm not."

———

The father offers his son a profound truth: God is the same *everywhere*. On street corners and school yards, in sanctuaries and soup kitchens, among sinners and saints. We need not go anywhere or do anything or be anyone else for the divine to delight in our daily lives.

The son offered his father a profound truth right back: the natural world teems with God's presence. Wandering in it *will* change us.

The prophet Isaiah writes of God's glory revealed in the created world: valleys filled in, mountains and hills made low, rugged land made plain. The way of the Lord is through the wilderness.

It makes sense for the wilderness to be a site of divine revelation. Wilderness reflects wildness—and ours is a wild God! What a wild thing for the Creator of the Universe to become human. To be born of a woman. To live and breathe on this earth. To suffer and die for our sake. To rise again in everlasting glory.

The way of the Lord is wild.

The way of the Lord is through the wilderness.

Meditation: Preparing for new life can pull us into the wilderness—both metaphorically and literally. The outdoors offers, among many gifts, space to wander and fresh air to stimulate thinking.

Take a contemplative walk. Find a path where you feel safe to slow down and reflect. What areas of your life feel wild right now? How are you experiencing God's presence?

Prayer: God of all wildness and wonder, you reveal your glory among mountains and valleys, rugged lands and rough country. Bless our natural world. Protect our seas and skies. Guide leaders across the world to take action to slow the climate crisis and care for our common home.

December 11: Wednesday of the Second Week of Advent

Promise of Rest

Readings: Isa 40:25-31; Matt 11:28-30

Scripture:
"Come to me, all you who labor and are burdened, and I will give you rest." (Matt 11:28)

Reflection: Today is for the birds.

My body sinks into a chocolate leather recliner at the local retreat center. I gaze through the glass door in front of me. Is that a sparrow pecking at the feeder? *The Sibley Guide to Birds* sits on the side table ready to consult. More likely a swallow. Western meadowlark to be exact—the yellow underbelly gives her away.

Two cawing crows make their presence known below. They startle the resident squirrel who scampers off in a huff. His frenetic energy reminds me of my own busy days.

But not today. Today is for slowing down. Today is for staring out the window and resting. Today is for the birds.

————

Jesus Christ carries the weight of the world on his shoulders. Still, he describes his burden as "light." Jesus moves from city to city, speaking to crowds of needy people. Still, his promise of rest remains.

How does Jesus do it?

Perhaps the key lies in his self-description: "I am meek and humble of heart." Throughout his ministry, Jesus takes seriously the limits of his human body. After full days of preaching and healing, Jesus retreats into the mountains alone. He once even napped on a boat in the middle of a storm!

Jesus models the way. What might it feel like to lean into Christ's promise of rest during busy December days? To entrust the Son of God with all that worries and wearies us? This Advent season, let us draw ever closer to the One who longs to restore us and make us whole.

Meditation: Preparing for new life ought to include rest. Even God took a break after creating the world! God blessed Sabbath time on the seventh day of creation—and every day thereafter. We are not made to be productivity machines.

Try taking a nap as a spiritual practice. Allow your body and mind to drift into gentle sleep. Prioritize regular times for rest and renewal throughout the Advent season.

Prayer: God of the Sabbath, you promise rest to those who are labored and burdened. Refresh the weary bodies of over-worked employees, caregivers, and all who struggle to find respite in their days.

December 12: Our Lady of Guadalupe

Who Are Your Elizabeths?

Readings: Zech 2:14-17 or Rev 11:19a; 12:1-6a, 10ab;
Luke 1:26-38 or 1:39-47

Scripture:
"And how does this happen to me, that the mother of my
Lord should come to me?" (Luke 1:43)

Reflection: Bottom of the ninth inning. Home team down
two. Runners on first and third. *Here comes Braun,* my old
friend mutters. *Hot bat. He'll get it done.*

We've been going to ballgames together for more than a
decade. I trust his commentary—about hot bats, cold shoulders, hard diagnoses, and everything else that matters.

Braun swings big on an inside fastball. *Craaack!*

"Get up! Get up! Get outta here . . . gone!" roars the radio
announcer behind us.

If heaven is having nowhere I'd rather be and no one I'd
rather be with, then tonight is a taste of the bliss to come.

———

Upon consenting to carry God's Son, Mary made her way
across the hill country to Elizabeth. She needed a safe space.
She needed a trusted confidant. She needed her beloved
cousin—and Elizabeth welcomed her with spirit.

"Most blessed are you among women!" Elizabeth exalts. Even the infant in her womb leaps in wonder. Joy envelops them both.

Who are the Elizabeths in your life? Those people you move toward with haste, who welcome you into their homes and hearts, who rejoice over the blessing that is your very being?

On this feast of Our Lady of Guadalupe, may the church especially celebrate the many Elizabeths in Latinx communities. Let us celebrate the dedicated faithful who witness to the power of meaningful relationships through love and service to community.

For all of our Elizabeths, past, present, and future: *Gracias a Dios*, thanks be to God!

Meditation: Preparing for new life can kindle deeper companionship. Creation rarely happens in a vacuum. We join with family, friends, neighbors, and even strangers in anticipation of what is to come.

Reach out to a friend you haven't connected with in a while. Set up a time to meet for coffee or talk on the phone. Rejoice in the gifts of connection.

Prayer: Ever-present God, you call your people into communion with one another. Grace each of us with Elizabeths in our lives who reflect your love and care.

Holy in Our Midst

Readings: Isa 48:17-19; Matt 11:16-19

Scripture:
I, the LORD, your God,
    teach you what is for your good . . . (Isa 48:17)

Reflection: You came to the shelter in search of warm socks and migraine medicine. Maybe a shower if the line isn't too long. Your head throbs. All you want is to fall asleep and forget this day. But you're on a mission: *Socks, check. Extra-strength Tylenol, check. Shower, not worth the wait.*

You hurry out to catch the last bus of the night. Not ten minutes later, you storm back into the shelter with tears streaking your frozen cheeks. "The driver drove right past me without even stopping!" You repeat over and over: "He didn't see me. Why didn't he see me?"

———

God teaches us what is for our good: to listen, to pay attention, to keep judgements at bay. The old adage warns that things are not always what they seem. First appearances can be deceptive. God's own Son lived among the least. Jesus took on the troubles of the lowly. John the Baptist did too, proclaiming the Good News with wild hair and tattered clothes.

The generation of people referenced in today's Gospel parable do not listen to John or Jesus. Like stubborn children, they refuse to pay attention to the outcasts. Instead, they claim John is possessed by a demon; they judge Jesus' friends.

What might it take to truly embrace the holy in our midst without judgement or reservation? To see others with the gentle eye of God? To prepare for a world where no one gets left behind?

Meditation: Preparing for new life offers plenty of opportunities to listen and learn from others. The new person, thing, or experience is likely to disrupt our routines. This can be an invitation to encounter the world anew and grow in appreciation for the people around us.

Notice those whose labor often goes unnoticed, like the clerk at your local grocery store or your parish's custodian. Thank them for their efforts.

Prayer: God of wisdom, you empower each of us to proclaim the Good News of Christ Jesus your Son. Make us conduits of your love to the ends of the earth.

Never Far Away

Readings: Sir 48:1-4, 9-11; Matt 17:9a, 10-13

Scripture:
"Elijah will indeed come and restore all things; but I tell you that Elijah has already come . . ." (Matt 17:11-12)

Reflection: "May those who have died find rest in God . . ."

The petition brings you back to your beloved. For a moment, he fills this sacred space once more. You sense his presence. His smile, his scent. The delight he found in fine wine and great books and you. Could it really be years since the morning he fell asleep for the final time with you by his side?

Blessed is he who enters eternity enveloped in love. Gone, but never far away. For while his body returned to dust, his spirit sings always in you.

————

The one who lived like fire entered heaven in a whirlwind of flames. Even death could not extinguish light so bright. Elijah left this earth—but his calling raged on.

Elijah's prophetic call raged on in Elisha. It raged on in John the Baptist. The great prophet's presence changed but was no less real after being assumed into heaven. One of the great mysteries of faith. Death *should* be the end. And yet.

We know the fate of the babe about to be born. Jesus suffers mightily. He dies a brutal death on the cross. Then the Son rises.

Jesus conquers death. His tomb becomes a womb for everlasting life. Death does not get the final say. The Son of God breathes new life into our ancestors, those who have fallen asleep in the hope of rising again.

Meditation: Preparing for new life can draw us closer to our loved ones. It is natural to reflect on what is and what has been as we get ready for what will be. The wisdom and spiritual presence of our ancestors provide a strong foundation from which to enter our next seasons. The line between heaven and earth is a thin one.

Visit a cemetery where a loved one is buried or light a candle in their memory. Look through old photos. Ask your beloved dead to intercede for you in the days ahead.

Prayer: God of our ancestors, you guide generations of people into meaningful lives of love and service. Embolden us to continue the legacy of those who have gone before us so we may be beacons of hope for today's world.

THIRD WEEK OF ADVENT

December 15: Third Sunday of Advent

Snack on Joy

Readings: Zeph 3:14-18a; Phil 4:4-7; Luke 3:10-18

Scripture:
Shout for joy, O daughter Zion! (Zeph 3:14)

Reflection: "All right, buddy, are you ready?" The young athlete sitting a few feet from me rocks back and forth in his wheelchair. He cannot talk but makes plenty of noise. He communicates mostly through grunts and giggles, his crystal blue eyes gazing around.

He can barely keep the glove on his hand—much less catch the ball—but that doesn't stop us from trying. Week after week, I push him out to centerfield and toss him the ball. Time after time, the ball hits his glove or the side of his wheelchair and rolls away.

Until today.

"Here it comes!" I shout as the ball leaves my hand. For the first time, the ball lands smack in the palm of his glove. Success!

Giddy, the outfielder grins and shrieks, blessing the ballpark with holy joy.

———

Christians near and far will soon cry out, "Joy to the world! The Lord is come!" The Third Sunday of Advent offers a foretaste of such joy.

The prophet Zephaniah paints a delightful image of God as dancing partner to daughter Zion. Enemies are expelled. Gloom turns to gladness. God and the people sing, exult, and dance with profound joy as if at a wedding feast. After years of suffering, it's time to celebrate.

What if the same holds true for us?

Let us give thanks on this Gaudete Sunday for our emotive God. May we too find comfort in the divine assurance that joy will always win out in the end.

Meditation: Laboring life into the world can elicit joy. Birth pangs mix with feelings of glad anticipation and accomplishment. *I did it! We did it!* What a marvel to behold new life. We are called into this joy of anticipation on Gaudete Sunday.

Try "snacking on joy" as *Washington Post* columnist Richard Sima puts it. Savor little bites of joy found in the ordinary—a compliment from a stranger, a particularly delicious meal, a breakthrough at work.

Prayer: Gracious God, stir a spirit of gladness within your people. Fill us with holy joy as we anticipate the Savior's birth.

Nevertheless, You Persist

Readings: Num 24:2-7, 15-17a; Matt 21:23-27

Scripture:
"By what authority are you doing these things?" (Matt 21:23)

Reflection: Persistence pulses through female bodies, a spark as natural as blood and breath. It drives us to dig deeper: *Come on, keep pushing. You've got this!* It doubles down on doubt: *Don't listen to them. You matter. You're worth it.* It dares us to dream big: *Think she can't do it? Think again!*

By what authority are you doing these things? The question no longer phases you. You're a woman. You've served the church for decades. If you had a dollar for every doubt, you could finally afford to take a vacation.

Nevertheless, you persist. You claim the authority bestowed upon you in baptism. With grit and grace, you pave the way for the next generation of ministers.

What an honor it is to stand on your shoulders.

––––––––––

The chief priests and elders question Jesus: "By what authority are you doing these things?" Their worldly understandings of power and privilege pale in comparison to the divine authority through which the Son of God speaks and acts. Jesus feels no need to prove himself to anyone. He does not thump his chest. While religious leaders gripe and grope for external validation, the Son of God claims his authority from within. He allows his actions to do the heavy lifting.

Jesus persists through declarations of doubt—and models a way forward for his followers. In this Advent season, may we too claim the authority God bestows on us through baptism and use it to better the world.

Meditation: Laboring life into the world draws forth the authority of the laborer. Other people can support the laborer to an extent. But when it comes time to push, there's only one person who can take the lead.

Mark out an hour on your calendar for you and God. Pray. Walk. Journal. Invest in yourself and your relationship with the One who creates and calls you.

Prayer: Persistent God, you never stop drawing out the gifts of your people. Animate all of our lives with meaning and purpose. Help us to recognize and claim the authority bestowed in baptism so we might be agents of healing in the world.

December 17: Tuesday of the Third Week of Advent

Learned from the Best

Readings: Gen 49:2, 8-10; Matt 1:1-17

Scripture:
The book of the genealogy of Jesus Christ, the son of David, the son of Abraham. (Matt 1:1)

Reflection: "They're here!" Lisa shrieks with Christmas joy, waking up to photos from the hospital. Her sister just delivered twins a few hundred miles away.

She hops in the car. Along the way, she thinks of her own beloved aunt. The woman who never missed a band concert or dance recital. The woman whose love made Lisa feel like she could walk on water.

Poet Maya Angelou once said, "I sustain myself with the love of family." So too does Lisa. And she is more than ready to envelop the next generation in that same faithful, familial love. After all, she learned from the best.

———

With each passing name, the genealogy of Jesus Christ draws us closer to the universe-tearing truth of Christmas: God became human. Fully divine became fully human, too.

Our great God entered humanity with all its flaws and foibles. God—*God!*—entered the history of the same world we call home. The Savior sprouted a branch on Abraham and Sarah's family tree. Rooted in the lineage of sinners and saints, Jesus Christ became one of us to save all of us—past, present, and future.

This year, let us listen with fresh hearts to the names of God's human family. Nahshon, Ruth, and Josiah: pray for us! Zadok, Jacob, and Mary: pray for us! And let us add our own names to the list. Dear grandma, cherished uncle, sweet daughter: pray for us! For God embraces everyone in the divine family tree.

Meditation: Laboring life into the world extends a family's lineage. The birth of a child is often an occasion for familial reflection. Who are this child's ancestors? Which family traits do we hope to pass on to this child—and which must be left behind?

Draw out your biological or chosen family tree. Reflect on the relationships sprouting from its branches. Consider reaching out to someone on the tree whom you have not connected with in a while.

Prayer: Compassionate God, you reveal the power of your divine love through your Son Jesus. Embolden us to spread that love in our homes and communities.

Raising Risk-Takers

Readings: Jer 23:5-8; Matt 1:18-25

Scripture:
"[D]o not be afraid to take Mary your wife into your home."
(Matt 1:20)

Reflection: You enter the living room to a familiar scene. Your biggest cheerleader reclines in the easy chair. Your staunchest supporter reads on the sofa.

Mom and Dad knew you before you took your first breath. They know your favorite foods, classmate dramas, and dreams for the future. They know everything about you. Except for one thing. One big thing.

You say a quick prayer that your parents will love you just the same as they did five minutes ago. With sweaty palms and a pounding heart, you step forward to speak your truth. "Mom, Dad, there's something I need to tell you . . ."

———

The angel assures Mary that God will be with her. Still, her "yes" is not without risk. Mary conceives Jesus while engaged—but not yet married—to Joseph. The future Mother of God will face great stigma and shame if word spreads that she is pregnant out of wedlock.

Mary says yes anyway.

The early Gospel narratives reveal God to be a risk-taker as well. Our almighty God could have picked any woman to fulfill what the prophets foretold. Yet God chose a poor girl from the country. What if she couldn't handle the pressure? Our all-powerful God does not need permission to act. Yet God asks Mary for consent. What if she had said no?

Inspired by God and Mary, may we too have the courage to take risks and to support those who have taken the risk of sharing themselves with us.

Meditation: Laboring life into the world can be risky. Complications arise in the delivery room. An idea faces pushback. There are no guarantees of an easy entrance into the world.

The words "breath" and "Spirit" are related. Practice breathing exercises to grow centered and to calm anxieties. Begin with square breathing: inhale for four seconds, hold for four seconds, exhale for four seconds, and hold for four seconds. Repeat at your own pace, resting in God's Spirit.

Prayer: Prophetic God, you raise up risk-takers to live out the compassionate, challenging word of Jesus. Protect us in times of exploration and uncertainty. Make your presence known when we need your companionship the most.

December 19: Thursday of the Third Week of Advent

Someday?

Readings: Judg 13:2-7, 24-25a; Luke 1:5-25

Scripture:
But they had no child, because Elizabeth was barren and both were advanced in years. (Luke 1:7)

Reflection: You've dreamed of it since girlhood. Since the days of trying on your mom's wedding dress and rocking your dolls to sleep. Family life calls to you.

Someday.

Years pass. Relationships come and go. Now reminders of what you want—and don't yet have—appear everywhere. Out for a walk, you pass an elderly couple holding hands. Over drinks with friends, you hear tales of family milestones and mishaps. You listen and laugh along. With a smile on your face and a sting in your heart, you wonder quietly if it will ever be your turn.

Someday?

———————

Eventually the hoped-for happens. Elizabeth conceives and bears a son. She becomes a mother for the first time late in life. But what about her many years of barrenness? What about those lonely nights of wishing and waiting and wondering?

The fact that Elizabeth conceives a child does not erase the fact that she spent nearly a lifetime longing for one. God understood her pain—and held her in the highest regard. Cultural norms and expectations of the day may have led Elizabeth to ask herself, "What good is a woman who cannot give her husband a child?"

In God's eyes: very good. God called Elizabeth "righteous." God recognized the goodness in this prophetic woman long before she bore the Baptist. God dwelled with Elizabeth and her husband, just as God dwells with each of us regardless of what we can or cannot do.

Meditation: Laboring life into the world is an experience longed for by many. Countless people dream of bringing new life into the world, only to have those dreams crushed by forces outside of their control. Living in a state of longing can feel isolating.

Fast from something meaningful to you for a day or a week. (The practice is not only reserved for Lent!) Let this experience draw you closer to those who go without.

Prayer: Merciful God, envelop in your tender love all people who ache with longing. Make your steadfast presence known in the hearts of all who are hurting.

December 20: Friday of the Third Week of Advent

Get Through Together

Readings: Isa 7:10-14; Luke 1:26-38

Scripture:
But she was greatly troubled at what was said . . .
(Luke 1:29)

Reflection: You see it coming from the top of the driveway.
Your brave boy takes too sharp a turn on his new scooter
and lands sideways in the grass.

"Waaaaahhhhh!" he screams as big tears streak his sweaty
face. Seconds later you scoop him into your arms—and the
wails turn to whimpers.

Mom's magic touch.

"Are you hurt or scared?" you ask with great tenderness.

After a few big sniffles, he whispers, "Scared."

"It's okay to be scared!" you affirm, stroking his curly
blond hair. "Mama gets scared too sometimes. We get
through the scary stuff together."

———

The young girl had every right to be "greatly troubled."

Wouldn't you be scared to see an angel? To be dubbed full
of grace? To learn the Lord is with you in some unique way?
Mary was just going about her day. She woke up, maybe ate
breakfast, took a walk. In the midst of her ordinary life,

the angel delivers to Mary a life-altering—earth-shaking, universe-bending—ask: to bear God's Son.

God's favor rests upon Mary. The brave girl believes the angel's message. There is no need to fear. Like a mother comforts her child, God through the angel assures Mary that the Spirit will be with her every step of the way. They will bring this most holy human life into the world together. They will take on the impossible together.

They will get through the scary stuff together.

Meditation: Laboring life into the world can be scary. We can only ready ourselves so much for the unknown. Nothing can truly prepare a person for all that awaits in the future—in part because each experience is unique. Is the laborer ready to grow and change? Are there others around to offer support? Even in the best circumstances, issues often arise in labor that prompt fear and anxiety.

Hold in prayer all those who are afraid or alone today.

Prayer: Almighty God, you never leave us to face our perils alone. Calm our anxious hearts and relieve our fears.

Time to Push

Readings: Song 2:8-14 or Zeph 3:14-18a; Luke 1:39-45

Scripture:
"Blessed are you who believed that what was spoken to you by the Lord would be fulfilled." (Luke 1:45)

Reflection: For nine months you prepared for this moment. Nine months of nausea and sciatica. Nine months of sleepless nights and swollen feet. Nine months of sharing your body with the little one in your belly.

"Pain is part of what it takes to grow a human," you reflect. Summoning all your strength, you take a deep breath and grip the rail of the hospital bed. The moment you prepared for, hoped for, dreamed about is here. New life is coming.

It's time to push.

———

Seasonal songs and images tend to depict Mary as meek. Mild and lowly. A passive mother cradling her newborn in a pristine barn. The scene suggests coziness and quiet.

But what about Mary's strength?

The Mother of God embodied incredible strength from the moment she heard the angel's amazing exaltation: "Hail, full of grace! The Lord is with you." Mary showed the strength to believe the unbelievable. The strength to trust an angel's message. The strength to carry a child in the womb. The strength to labor a child into the world. The strength to raise a child and love that child and later let go of that child so that he might fulfill his calling.

Mary stayed by her child's side all the way to the cross. She heard his agonized cries. She saw the bruises and blood covering his body. She did the hardest thing a parent can ever do as she watched her beloved son take his final breath.

Meek Mary? Not so much.

Meditation: Laboring life into the world takes enormous strength. The physical act of giving birth is an incredible feat in and of itself. What comes next is just as demanding. Raising a child calls forth the full attention of a parent, especially in the early years.

Offer to drop off a meal to a family in your parish or community with young kids. If you know the family well, offer to watch the kids for an hour so the parent(s) can rest. Acknowledge the hard, holy labor of family life.

Prayer: Laboring God, you partner with Mary to bring your Son into the world. Bless and strengthen all parents as they live into the vocation of parenthood.

FOURTH WEEK OF ADVENT

Channels of Blessing

Readings: Mic 5:1-4a; Heb 10:5-10; Luke 1:39-45

Scripture:
"Blessed are you among women, and blessed is the fruit of your womb." (Luke 1:42)

Reflection: *May God bless you and keep you safe and happy and healthy all the days of your long, long life. Amen. May you have sweet dreams and sleep all the night 'til the morning light. Amen.*

The words of my childhood bedtime blessing washed over me like a wave of relief. No matter what the day brought—a scraped knee, a bad grade, a recess spent alone—I believed it would all be okay come night, when Mom would turn off the lights, sit on the edge of my bed, and ask for God's blessings.

———

God could have called on priests to proclaim the Messiah's coming. God could have orchestrated an elaborate ritual to mark the Savior's impending birth. Instead, God's Spirit fills two pregnant women in the hill country. One unwed, another well past child-bearing years. Unlikely prophets prompted by the Holy Spirit to share Good News. To *feel* Good News dance in their wombs.

Elizabeth declares the Christ child as "Lord"—she is the first human being in the Gospels to make this confession

(Luke 1:43). A conduit of the Holy Spirit, Elizabeth blesses Mary and her unborn son with joyful energy and wondrous amazement. She gives voice to the stirrings of her heart. In doing so, Elizabeth reflects God's own delight in blessing new life and old life and all life in between.

Ours is a God of abundant blessings. Like Elizabeth and Mary, may we embrace the Spirit's blessings within ourselves and be channels of those blessings for all we meet.

Meditation: Beholding new life is a profound blessing. The opportunity to bear witness to life in its tiniest, tenderest moments is cause for celebration and reflection. How will this new being change our lives? Change the world?

Write a blessing for something new in your life. This could be anything from a new relationship or creative project to a new biking route or house plant. Ask God to make the divine presence known in the new.

Prayer: Devoted God, pour out your Spirit upon your beloved world. Bless us and keep us. Shine your face upon us and be gracious to us. Grant us peace.

Possibilities Abound

Readings: Mal 3:1-4, 23-24; Luke 1:57-66

Scripture:
"What, then, will this child be?" (Luke 1:66)

Reflection: The long-awaited envelope arrives in the mail on a chilly spring day. With shaking hands, you trace the familiar logo of your dream college. What lies inside will chart the course of your next four years. Your heart pounds like a jackhammer.

"Congratulations! You've been admitted!" reads the first line. Your face flushes. A cocktail of joy and relief—and trepidation—floods your teenage body. Accepting this offer means moving away from home. Saying goodbye to friends. Growing up. What will the next four years hold? Who will you become?

———

God creates generously. Possibilities abound in the divine imagination. The womb of a woman thought to be barren carries a child. A man who could not hear or speak regains his senses. A newborn reflects God's favor to the Israelites.

Fear and amazement come upon the neighbors bearing witness to the God of possibilities. Word spreads throughout the hill country: Be watchful. Be alert. Incredible things are starting to take place. Of John the people wonder, "What, then, will this child be?" This child, cradled in the hand of the Lord. This child, full of potential. This child, brimming with hope. Who will he become?

Similar questions swirl around the one who comes next. Who will God Incarnate be? What will the Messiah do? How will his reign change the course of human history? Possibilities emerge for the people Israel—and the whole of creation—from the births of Jesus and John.

Meditation: Beholding new life can fill us with hope and possibilities. Potential overflows, especially in the early days. What now? What's next? What could be?

Allow yourself to dream big. Gift yourself the space to imagine without inhibition. Silence the voices that say, "You can't" or "That's not possible." Instead, lean into your hopes. What would you do—who would you be—if anything were possible?

Prayer: God of surprises, you bring forth life from the womb of a woman thought to be barren. Stir up hope within us. Help us to be people of possibility and potential.

God Is With Us

Readings: 2 Sam 7:1-5, 8b-12, 14a, 16; Luke 1:67-79

Scripture:
[A]nd they shall name him Emmanuel, / which means "God is with us." (Matt 1:23; Christmas Vigil Mass)

Reflection: *God is with us.*

In the newborn wailing in the back pew and her brother clamoring for attention, *God is with us.*

In the ragtag choir belting "Gloria" only slightly offkey, *God is with us.*

In the usher who has served for half a century and the liturgist scurrying about, *God is with us.*

In the devoted church ladies and nervous boyfriends, *God is with us.*

In the teens who aren't excited but show up anyway, *God is with us.*

In the passing of peace and pardoning of sins, *God is with us.*

In the bread being broken and wine poured out, *God is with us.*

This is the night. The night to behold the chosen child, the Christ, Emmanuel. The night to celebrate the universe-bending truth that right here, right now, *God is with us.*

———————

May we take a few moments tonight to grow quiet and revel in the mystery of the Incarnation. The great inbreaking. The night when a young country girl gives birth to God's own Son. Divinity takes on humanity. The Chosen One becomes a vulnerable newborn. The Savior of the Universe gets swaddled and nursed and changed and nursed again. Christmas changes everything.

On this holiest of nights, let us give thanks for all that was and all that is and all that will be. Emmanuel is here now—and Emmanuel will come once more. Forever and always, *God is with us.*

Meditation: Beholding new life reminds us that God is with us. God's own Son was once small and vulnerable. God blesses those sacred, early moments when hopes become realities and nothing will ever be the same again.

Go to Mass tonight if you are able. Encounter the living God present in the gathered community, the Body of Christ. Encounter the living God in the gifts of the altar, the bread and wine. Encounter the living God in the words of Sacred Scripture. Embrace the greatest gift of all: *God is with us.*

Prayer: Generous God, you brought your Son into the world to be one with your beloved creation. Inspire us to spread the hope of Christmas to everyone we meet.

SEASON OF CHRISTMAS

December 25: The Nativity of the Lord (Christmas)

Light Lives Among Us

Readings:
VIGIL: Isa 62:1-5; Acts 13:16-17, 22-25; Matt 1:1-25 or
    1:18-25
NIGHT: Isa 9:1-6; Titus 2:11-14; Luke 2:1-14
DAWN: Isa 62:11-12; Titus 3:4-7; Luke 2:15-20
DAY: Isa 52:7-10; Heb 1:1-6; John 1:1-18 or 1:1-5, 9-14

Scripture:
The true light, which enlightens everyone, was coming into
the world. (John 1:9)

Reflection: I watch in awe as fifteen-foot flames shoot out of
the chimney of the largest wood-fired kiln in North America.
Streaks of yellow, orange, and red paint the midnight sky.
The smell of smoke lingers in the air. If it weren't so danger-
ous, I would remove my shoes. For where I'm standing is
holy ground.

"This all started with a single match," chuckles a veteran
potter as he reaches up to touch his charred eyebrows. "Ain't
it amazing what a spark can become?!"

With each stoke of wood the fire gains more energy. Flames
dance around thousands of pieces of pottery nestled care-
fully inside the kiln. Unique patterns decorate each ceramic
surface. In a few weeks, the potters will unseal the kiln and
marvel at the beauty of their creations.

· But for now, on this holy night, the fire has more work to do.

———————

The Light of the World dwelled with the Creator and the Spirit from the very beginning. A generative Trinity giving life and love to all things. It was good.

Then sin happened. Humanity fell. We needed help. We needed a savior. The Light could not stay away. "He was in the world," John writes of God's Son (1:9). Born of a woman. Born on a stable floor. God's own Son took on the messiness of flesh.

On this Christmas Day, let us rejoice in the truth that the Light of the World lived among us—and the Spirit of Light still lives among us! Glory to God in the highest!

Meditation: Beholding new life lights up the world. Flickers of hope and possibility brighten once empty spaces. People encountering new life often come away glowing. What a precious gift! What an exciting start!

Give yourself a nice candle for Christmas. Begin or end the day in candlelight. Bring the image of Christ as the Light of the World to life in the quiet of your own home.

Prayer: God of light and life, you sent your Son into the world out of great love for your creation. Fill us with the joy of Christmas as we glory in the Savior's birth.

Hope of Resurrection

Readings: Acts 6:8-10; 7:54-59; Matt 10:17-22

Scripture:
"Behold, I see the heavens opened . . ." (Acts 7:56)

Reflection: As soon as the big wooden clock strikes nine, you lift your hand to your forehead and pray: *In the name of the Father, and of the Son, and of the Holy Spirit. Amen.*

Cancer courses through your 96-year-old body—but this grandma won't miss the televised Sunday service. You know your time on earth is almost up. But you know something else too: soon you will join the chorus of ancestors who have fallen asleep in the hope of the resurrection. For nearly a century, you have professed belief in a God who conquers death. You know the stories of resurrection in your bones. You have been nourished by the bread of life and the cup of salvation tens of thousands of times. You believe in their saving power.

———

God welcomes our beloved dead into the glory of eternal life. Martyrs, grandmothers, the lost and lonely, the old and the young—God treasures everyone. God's Son lived and died to save us all.

Through the mystery of Christ's dying and rising, we learn the tomb was never meant to mark an ending. Rather, God raised Jesus to new, everlasting life. Our Lord ascended into heaven and sits at the right hand of the Almighty. He continues to intercede for us. He continues to be made known to us in the breaking of the bread, in the drinking of the cup, in each of us, and in our beloved dead.

May the souls of all the departed, through the mercy of God, rest in gentle peace.

Meditation: Beholding new life can trigger memories of those beloved people who now live with God in heaven. Older generations pass on while new generations join the family. We say goodbye to some loved ones while saying hello to others. The cycle of life can be both cruel and compassionate.

Place a framed photo of a deceased loved one on your dining table. Recall your favorite Christmas memories together.

Prayer: God of wisdom, grant peace to all people in their final days. Fill them with resurrection hope, and when their time comes, welcome them into the joys of everlasting life with you.

December 27: Saint John the Apostle

Cascade of Emotions

Readings: 1 John 1:1-4; John 20:1a, 2-8

Scripture:
On the first day of the week, Mary Magdalene ran . . .
(John 20:1)

Reflection: It was a day to remember. It was a day to forget.
I crumpled onto the couch as the sun set, exhausted and
emotional in the face of a family crisis. The friend who came
over to keep me company didn't know what else to do, so
he sat down, and he cried, too.

———————

Her dear friend had just died a dreadful death. Hours
earlier, Mary of Magdala watched as Jesus cried out from
the cross and breathed his last. Now she returns to the burial
site to mourn. It does not take long for her eyes to adjust to
the darkness of early morning. What she sees astounds her.
The stone that sealed the tomb—the stone that separated
what was from what is—has been removed. How? The stone
had seemed impossible to budge. It was meant to mark an
ending.

But this death is different.

The cascade of emotions coursing through Mary's body at
this moment must have been torrential. Shock: *What is happening right now?* Anger: *Who had the audacity to take the Lord*

from the tomb? Despair: *These days have been dreadfully sad . . . now this?* Grief: *I would give anything to have my friend back.*

As darkness turns to dawn on the first day of the week, Mary finds herself at the threshold of love's greatest mystery. Feeling the heaviest of feelings, her body easily could have crumbled under the weight of grief. She could have stood still. She could have sat down. Instead, Mary runs. She surges ahead and proclaims with her whole self: *This death is different!*

Meditation: Beholding new life can prompt all kinds of emotions. Humans are not programmed to react in a set way to any given circumstance. Some approach new life with fear and anxiety. Others run toward it with joy and relief.

What emotions are you carrying today? Take special note of the parts of your body holding tension. How might you respond to this tension? Are you being called to restfulness or action?

Prayer: Emotive God, guide our thoughts, feelings, and actions toward you so we might reflect your glory to everyone we encounter.

How Long, O Lord?

Readings: 1 John 1:5–2:2; Matt 2:13-18

Scripture:
[Herod] ordered the massacre of all the boys in Bethlehem and its vicinity . . . (Matt 2:16)

Reflection: "All right everyone, it's time to put your phones in the basket," you announce at the beginning of your sixth period class. You have little patience for teens glued to technology.

You are about to begin the lesson when you spot a hot pink phone sticking out of the backpack of a girl in the last row. "Kids these days," you mumble as you walk over to the culprit. "What is that phone still doing with you?"

"I can't let it go," your young student whispers. "How will I call my mom if a shooter comes in?" Her answer haunts you to this day.

———

The church remembers and mourns the little ones slaughtered by order of King Herod on this feast of the Holy Innocents. The Son of God was barely out of the womb when he started receiving death threats. Herod was so hell-bent on preserving his power—so jealous and fearful of the changes to come—that he demanded death for this babe fresh from the manger. As the government hunted down Jesus, they killed other children in nearby regions.

Children massacred. *How long, O Lord?*

Today's difficult Gospel passage ends with the sounds of utter agony. A mother, inconsolable, sobbing and lamenting with her whole being for her children who would be no more. Through Rachel's weeping, we gain a glimpse of how God feels when God's beloved creation suffers. God laments the violence human beings inflict upon each other—then and now. God weeps, too.

How many lives must be lost to find a new way?

Meditation: Beholding new life can inspire us to create a safer world. Children deserve the chance to flourish. They deserve safe spaces to grow up and explore. In a world plagued by violence, what would it look like to demand a different future?

Is there a concrete way you can support young people in your parish or local community? Share your wisdom and unconditional love. Advocate for a safer future for all.

Prayer: God of peace and goodness, raise up prophetic voices in civic leadership who advocate for the health and safety of children. Bring a swift end to violence in our classrooms and communities.

December 29: The Holy Family of Jesus, Mary, and Joseph

Twisted in Knots

Readings: Sir 3:2-6, 12-14; Col 3:12-21 or 3:12-17;
Luke 2:41-52 *or, in Year C*, 1 Sam 1:20-22, 24-28; 1 John 3:1-2,
21-24; Luke 2:41-52

Scripture:
"Your father and I have been looking for you with great
anxiety." (Luke 2:48)

Reflection: You let out a long, labored sigh. Clothes and
books litter your bedroom floor. Photos from field trips and
soccer games hang from the walls. Your favorite stuffed
animal still sits atop the dresser. You have so much of your
childhood left to pack before tomorrow's big move out of
your parents' house and into your first apartment. Your
stomach twists in anxious knots.

*Will Mom and Dad be okay without me? What if I'm not ready
to be on my own? Why does time move so fast?*

———

Panic ensues when Mary and Joseph realize their pre-teen
son is nowhere to be found. Even the Son of God caused his
parents to worry! Today's Gospel tosses aside unrealistic images of the Holy Family living a perfect life. Mary and Joseph
lost Jesus. It took them a day to realize their son was missing
and another three days to find him back in Jerusalem.

Jesus' time in the temple was a turning point for the trio. Jesus separates from his parents, both literally and figuratively. He's growing up. So too are Mary and Joseph. They learn from their child just as much as their child learns from them.

The early lesson: change can be hard. New is not always nice and neat. Jesus' divine callings will lead him far beyond the family home. He will call his parents to adapt, to move through their anxieties and stretch into the fullness of their next holy chapter.

Meditation: Beginning again with new life can cause anxiety. Change disrupts. It is natural to worry about what lies ahead. How will this new being or development impact my life? What will happen to my cherished routines and plans?

Shift your focus to the realities of the present. God is here. Engage your five senses. What do you see? Hear? Feel? Smell? Taste?

Prayer: Loving God, you guided and inspired the Holy Family in their times of need. Through the love and intercession of Jesus, Mary, and Joseph, calm our anxieties and help us to be people of peace.

She Showed Up

Readings: 1 John 2:12-17; Luke 2:36-40

Scripture:
She never left the temple, but worshiped night and day . . .
(Luke 2:37)

Reflection: On an overcast summer evening, hope showed up wearing a pair of orthotic shoes.

To her left was the town harbor. To her right was a city park that had echoed its share of gunshots in recent months. Dozens of people convened in the park that night to walk silently in the name of peace. Most were young and able-bodied. They thought nothing of moving a mile in quiet protest. But toward the back was an older woman for whom mobility was not a given.

She shuffled and labored for each step. The heels of her walker grinded against the pavement. Surely her feet ached.

And still, she showed up.

———

The prophetess Anna held out hope that she would see God face-to-face. For years Anna worshiped in the temple day and night. She showed up. She persisted in faith. Standing on the shoulders of Deborah, Miriam, and other female prophets, Anna staked her faith in God. She believed in

God's faithfulness to the promises made to God's people—and she lived to see those promises fulfilled in the sweet baby resting before her.

Anna's faithful witness reminds us that God too is faithful. Always. God's word can be trusted. God will bring to fulfillment the promises made long ago. The lost will be found. The lowly will be lifted. Mercy and justice, love and light, will one day reign supreme.

Meditation: Beginning again with new life can call to mind the significance of showing up. God shows up on street corners and in sanctuaries, on park benches and in parish pews. God broadens the definition of sacred spaces. Anywhere can be holy if we bring our true selves to it.

Go to a special place that is accessible to you today. Consider a favorite picnic table, a corner of your apartment, or a local chapel. Bless the space with your presence. Know that God is there too. Take your shoes off if you can. Feel the holy ground beneath you.

Prayer: Courageous God, bless us with boldness to show up where your love is needed most.

Make Room

Readings: 1 John 2:18-21; John 1:1-18

Scripture:
And the Word became flesh
   and made his dwelling among us . . . (John 1:14)

Reflection: How easy it is to hurry through the world. One of my most vivid college memories is from an entirely ordinary day. I emerged from my fifth meeting of the morning as the campus bells struck noon. With just five minutes to spare, I powered on to my spiritual direction appointment with the force of a determined mall-walker.

"What I wouldn't give for a few extra hours!" I bemoaned as I pushed through my director's door, panting and frazzled.

The sweet sister looked up from her desk and smiled. "God graces everyone with the same amount of time in a day," she remarked. "It's up to you to make room."

———

The divine dwells among us. God dwells within our hearts and homes. God dwells amid neighbors and strangers. God dwells in spite of our sins and shortcomings. God dwells beyond our wildest dreams—here, there, everywhere.
The divine dwells among us.

The Word became flesh. The divine took up space in this world out of great love for us. How might we reciprocate even an ounce of that holy love back to God? Healthy relationships require effort from both parties. God chose to dwell with us. What might it look like for us to choose to dwell with God?

These tender Christmas days invite us to make room in our minds and hearts, to set aside distractions so we might deepen our relationship with the divine.

Meditation: Beginning again with new life requires us to make room. New beings need space to exist and grow. They need supportive environments where it is safe to try and fail and try again. How might we make room for new life in this new year? What might we need to let go of in order to free our hearts for whatever—or whoever—comes next?

Practice making room by cleaning out a closet or drawer in your living space. Say goodbye to the things that no longer serve you. Donate what might be useful to someone else.

Prayer: Expansive God, make our hearts malleable so we might welcome new people and experiences with your generous grace.

Treasure These Things

Readings: Num 6:22-27; Gal 4:4-7; Luke 2:16-21

Scripture:
And Mary kept all these things, reflecting on them in her heart. (Luke 2:19)

Reflection: Ambulances whiz by as I linger in the hospital parking lot after our visit. When I was a child, I would sprint to the street corner to await your arrival. I would jump and twirl with excitement as your car appeared down the block. You would honk and wave through the open windows: "Hi, Princess! How's Dad's favorite girl?!"

I beamed with joy then—and I beam with joy now. I don't know how much time we have left together, but I treasure every moment in my heart.

———————

Mary pushes a baby out of her body—a feat that demands an immediate, intense presence in the moment. Then, while still sore and sweaty, the brand-new mom greets a group of shepherds who come to praise the newborn king. Such hospitality once again calls Mary to a particular presence in the here and now.

Still, the Mother of God makes space to reflect. She does not allow precious postpartum moments to fly by without treasuring them in her heart.

God creates us with the capacity to remember. Our bodies carry stories from the past and present into the future. At the start of this new year, we do well to follow Mary's model and allow our own hearts the space to reflect—to remember—as God intended.

Meditation: Beginning again with new life can evoke reflections and memories. What are significant milestones that led to now? Who are the wisdom figures who helped guide you to this moment?

Get together with a friend during one of these early January days. Slowly reflect together on the last year. What were your highs and lows? What were important moments of insight or challenge? Entrust the past to God.

Then look to the year ahead. How do you want to commit to living? Who will receive your time and energy? When and how will you make space for God?

Prayer: God of beginnings, bless us with good health and happiness in the year ahead. May our lives reflect your mercy and love.

EPIPHANY AND
BAPTISM OF THE LORD

January 2: Saints Basil the Great and Gregory Nazianzen

Power of Questions

Readings: 1 John 2:22-28; John 1:19-28

Scripture:
"What are you then? Are you Elijah?" (John 1:21)

Reflection: "Jessie, when is tomorrow?"

Years of studies did not prepare me to answer the question you shout from atop the playground slide on a hot summer afternoon. I furrow my brow and gaze off into the distance. *How does one explain time? What is time? Why does time move so fast?*

By the time I snap out of my philosophical musings, you're already down the slide and making a beeline for the swing set. I don't have an answer to your question, but you don't seem to mind. Aren't questions more powerful than answers anyway?

———

The priests and Levites pepper John with questions about his identity: *Who are you? Are you Elijah? Are you the Prophet? What do you have to say for yourself?*

John could have cut off their queries. He could have rolled his eyes and stormed away, annoyed by the priests' persistence. Instead, John sticks with them. He responds to each ask. He acknowledges the curiosity of the people in front of him.

John's patience reflects God's welcoming approach to questions. God welcomes our musings. God sticks with us in our uncertainty. God practices endless patience as we work through challenges and wrestle with life's many unknowns.

Questions should not immediately be interpreted as signs of doubt. Rather, questions can draw us deeper into the divine mystery. Wonder and awe make a great pair.

Let us not be afraid in this new year to bring our questions to God in prayer.

Meditation: Beginning again with new life can prompt many questions. Human beings are naturally curious creatures. The start of something new may make us wonder: *Why is this happening? What comes next? How will I change?*

Write out the questions you have for God. Be honest. Trust that God can handle whatever is on your heart. Remember that God's answers most likely will not arrive in our preferred format or timing—but this does not mean God is sitting idly by.

Prayer: God of curious hearts, receive with mercy the questions stirring in us. Grant us patience in times of uncertainty, and help us feel your abiding presence among us.

Slow Down, Honey!

Readings: 1 John 2:29–3:6; John 1:29-34

Scripture:
[W]hat we shall be has not yet been revealed. (1 John 3:2)

Reflection: I have one of those Big Life Things to figure out, so I head to the woods. Isn't God supposed to reveal Important Life Lessons on contemplative walks along scenic trails? If only the divine were that romantic!

I trudge through a miserable concoction of sleet and snow for twenty minutes before turning around, chilled to the bone and even less enlightened than when I began. With my car in sight, I try to take a shortcut over what I think is a sturdy snowbank. My leg sinks waist deep into the drift.

Across the parking lot, a woman leans against her snowmobile, chuckles, and takes a drag of her cigarette. "Slow down, honey!" she puffs. "Life ain't kind to those who hurry through it!"

———

God reveals over time. The call to be patient, to "trust in the slow work of God" as Pierre Teilhard de Chardin, SJ, writes, can be one of the more difficult calls of the Christian life. Many of us want direction and clarity. We want God to show us the way, preferably with a detailed itinerary!

Yet today's reading from the first letter of Saint John reminds us that "what we shall be has not yet been revealed." Revelation happens slowly, with time and trust. We cannot see how all the pieces of life's puzzle fit together, but we can rest in the assurance that we are God's beloved children.

God will never leave us to trudge through life's snowbanks alone.

Meditation: Beginning again with new life invites us to practice patience. We will surely not have everything figured out at the onset. What kinds of support might we need to live into the unknowns?

In times of uncertainty, slow yourself down and practice some deep breathing. Take a few long inhales, hold your breath for a few seconds, and then let out a long, loud exhale. Acknowledge what is in your control and what is left up to God.

Prayer: Almighty God, you sent your beloved Son into the world to be one with humankind. Strengthen our faith in your steadfast presence among us.

January 4: Saint Elizabeth Ann Seton

All In

Readings: 1 John 3:7-10; John 1:35-42

Scripture:
[Jesus] said to them, "Come, and you will see." (John 1:39)

Reflection: "Time out! Hey Ref, time out!" Coach yells across the gym. My teammates and I hustle to the sidelines. Sweat drips off our flushed faces. Down four points with two minutes left. Coach scribbles an inbounds play on the whiteboard, then gazes intensely around the huddle. "Now is the time to dig deep!" he yells with passion. "Now is the time to leave everything you've got on the court!"

The referee blows her whistle to resume play. We raise our hands together in the middle of the huddle.

"All in on three!" Coach shouts. "One, two, three . . ."

"All in!"

Jesus calls his followers to be all in.

John sparks intrigue in his disciples when he proclaims Jesus to be the "Lamb of God." The disciples approach Jesus and ask him a layered question: "Rabbi . . . where are you staying?" The disciples wonder not only about Jesus' physical location but also his proximity to God.

Jesus tells them, "Come, and you will see." He invites those disciples—and all of us—to draw closer to God. Come, and see. Come, and hear. Come, and feel the divine presence all around.

Jesus wants his followers to deepen their relationships with the source of all goodness and life. He wants us to commit to living lives of holiness and hope. We will be asked to leave a lot behind to follow Christ. Yet by going all in, we will gain more than we can ever imagine.

Meditation: Beginning again with new life can be a time to go all in. Newness necessitates change. Rather than run from it, why not dive headfirst into the possibilities? God did not create life to be lived half-heartedly. Instead, God calls us to embrace the new with full body, mind, and soul.

Resolve to put away devices and other distractions for an hour—or more. Focus on the task at hand at home or at work. Be fully present to the ideas, the work, or the people in front of you.

Prayer: God of glory, you sent your only Son into the world to strengthen and save your beloved creation. Imbue us with your Spirit so we might live life to the fullest.

Pay Attention

Readings: Isa 60:1-6; Eph 3:2-3a, 5-6; Matt 2:1-12

Scripture:
"We saw his star at its rising and have come to do him homage." (Matt 2:2)

Reflection: Have you ever listened to fresh ice make its way across a lake? One of my favorite winter spots is the shore of Lake Sagatagan in Collegeville, Minnesota. Bundled head to toe, I stand where land and frozen water meet, take a few deep breaths, and listen closely.

The spreading ice sounds like far-off fireworks on the Fourth of July. It sounds like crackling flames on the first night of a wood-kiln firing. I bring my ears closer to the ground. The ice sounds like a chorus of Rice Krispies dancing in milk. *Snap! Crackle! Pop!*

January days by the lake remind me to tune in. God, revealed all over the place in the natural world, charges us—with full body, mind, and soul—to pay attention.

The magi followed a star to find the Light of the World. These prophetic messengers studied astrology. They knew what to look for and where to look for it. But more importantly, the magi reverenced the night sky as a great divine tapestry. They understood the star as a physical sign of God's outpouring of light into the universe through the birth of a king. They entrusted their journey to the map above—and soon found themselves face-to-face with Jesus the Christ.

On this feast of the Epiphany of the Lord, may we also let God's signs scattered throughout the natural world draw us closer to Christ.

Meditation: As we journey through life, God calls us to pay attention. Saint Benedict got it right when he wrote in his Rule: "We believe the divine presence is everywhere." The entire universe teems with divine presence. We need only open our senses to recognize God all around.

Slow your body down today. Don't rush. Move with intention. Read, cook, walk, or wheel at half your usual pace. Pay attention to the gifts of creation around you and savor them.

Prayer: God of the universe, you gift us with your divine presence everywhere. Heighten our senses so we might grow ever more aware of your existence, everywhere we go and in everything we do.

Love Without Bounds

Readings: 1 John 3:22–4:6; Matt 4:12-17, 23-25

Scripture:
[A]nd they brought to him all who were sick with various diseases and racked with pain . . . (Matt 4:24)

Reflection: You press a cool washcloth against my burning forehead. "It'll be okay, honey," you promise. "Just try to sleep." My body shivers and shakes. Minutes turn to hours. You leave only to refresh the now warm washcloth in the bathroom sink across the hall.

"Mom's here," you whisper gently. "Everything is going to be okay." As always, you're right. The fever finally breaks in the middle of the night. Still, you don't leave my side until morning.

You're not a magician. You can't get rid of the things that make me sick or sad with the wave of a wand. But you are a healer. Your presence makes all the difference.

———

Today's Gospel showcases the Son of God's power to cure "every disease and illness among the people." Some may hear this story and rejoice. People received a second chance at life! Others may feel jealous. Such miraculous healing stories beg big questions: Why does Jesus not cure all people?

Why does suffering exist if our God is all-powerful? How come my prayers aren't being answered?

Jesus' ways are utterly mysterious. We won't get clean, clear answers to faith's biggest questions anytime soon. Still, we can be assured that Jesus heals all. Sickness and suffering may not be eliminated in our time on earth, but Jesus promises to make each of us whole again one day. Jesus promises to be a healing presence in our times of need and to restore all of us to the fullness of life.

Meditation: As we journey through life, God calls us to be a healing presence for others. We become what we receive in the Eucharist—a source of hope and new life. We are then sent forth into the world to proclaim Christ's healing with our lives.

Visit a loved one or neighbor who is suffering from a physical or mental health issue. Be a source of comfort and companionship. You need not do anything special. Your presence is gift enough.

Prayer: Mothering God, lay your healing touch upon all people in need of love and care.

Discipleship Demands

Readings: 1 John 4:7-10; Mark 6:34-44

Scripture:
"Give them some food yourselves." (Mark 6:37)

Reflection: "Could we bring you some food on Saturday? We can just drop it off if you need space and rest. We love you very much!"

Your message brings tears to my eyes. It's been a hard few weeks. But here you are, offering to drive more than two hours to bring me a container full of chili, a loaf of homemade bread, and the world's warmest hugs.

The food hasn't entered my stomach yet, but already I feel nourished.

———

Jesus feeds the hungry—and demands we do the same. His disciples urge Jesus to dismiss the hungry crowds so they can "buy themselves something to eat." The Son of God doesn't think this solution is good enough. "Give them some food yourselves," Jesus replies. He puts the onus on the disciples to ensure their neighbors have what they need.

Today's Gospel reminds us that Christ's way is a communal way. He sends his disciples then and now into the world to be people of service. Each encounter with another person, each hungry mouth fed, each call answered, each forgiveness granted, each injustice challenged, offers the opportunity to grow in love of neighbor.

Five loaves and two fish feeding hundreds is certainly the headlining miracle in today's Gospel. Yet in a world where "me first" mentalities often prevail, let us also marvel at the beauty of people looking out for one another and making sure that everyone has the nourishment needed to thrive.

Meditation: As we journey through life, God calls us to feed others. There is only one Messiah—and we are not him. We are, however, responsible for our neighbors. As Saint Paul taught, when one part of the Body suffers, all the parts suffer with it (1 Cor 12:26).

Make an extra dish of your favorite comfort food. Drop it off to a busy friend or a young family without expecting anything in return. If you don't know anyone who needs help with food, reach out to your parish or local food pantry for suggestions.

Prayer: Generous God, nourish us with the bread of life, cup of salvation, and fruits of the earth. Rid the world of hunger and other evils that leave people hurting.

Hermit Time

Readings: 1 John 4:11-18; Mark 6:45-52

Scripture:
[H]e went off to the mountain to pray. (Mark 6:46)

Reflection: Hermits today live everywhere—monastery cells, secluded cabins, and apparently, college frat houses.

Words like *asceticism* and *desert fathers* are nothing more than standardized test stumpers to Andrew and his roommates. Yet in their late teenage wisdom, they developed a code phrase with ancient roots: *I need some hermit time.*

When any roommate calls for "hermit time," it is understood that he will go into his room and shut the door. Sometimes for ten minutes. Sometimes for ten hours. Regardless, this roommate is not to be disturbed until he reemerges. No exceptions. No questions. Just time and space to recharge.

————

Jesus withdrew to the mountain alone. After feeding and healing and teaching and preaching to crowds of people, the Son of God needed to take a breath.

He needed some hermit time.

Jesus recognized the importance of pausing and praying. His body embraced times of rest and retreat. Contemplative practices sustained Jesus' ministry. Taking time away enabled the Son of God to meet the deluge of demands put upon him. Yet too often, such practices get lost in the bustle of daily life. Even in today's Gospel, it could be easy to miss the mention of Jesus' time alone on the mountain. The story is bookended by the flashier feeding of the five thousand and the calming of the sea.

Let us take the example set by Jesus—and these college students—into the new year. May our schedules reflect the value of "hermit time" for monastics and non-monastics alike.

Meditation: As we journey through life, there are times when God invites—or challenges—us to withdraw. Daily life demands a lot from each of us. To-do lists never stop growing. Our callings pull us in many directions—a reality that makes the practice of withdrawing even more necessary.

Plan out some time alone in the coming weeks. It could be a few hours at your local library or a weekend at a retreat center. Gift yourself time and space with God.

Prayer: God of the Sabbath, refresh us with times of silence and solitude. Quiet our hearts and give us space to withdraw into your gentle care.

Blessed Returns

Readings: 1 John 4:19–5:4; Luke 4:14-22a

Scripture:
Jesus returned to Galilee in the power of the Spirit . . .
(Luke 4:14)

Reflection: A squeak of the old front door hinge announces my presence. The school secretary, who generations of students have affectionately called "Mama," twists from her perch behind the welcome desk. "Well hi, Jessie!" Mama exclaims with the same energy she exuded fifteen years ago on my first day of high school. "It's so good to see you again! How's your mom? How's your brother?"

She remembers. Her eager greeting warms my heart. We catch up on the latest news, and as the conversation winds down, I take a big inhale—and chuckle. "The hallways still smell the same!" I observe.

Mama laughs, "Welcome home! Some things will never change!

———

Jesus returns to Galilee, guided by the power of the Holy Spirit. After overcoming temptation in the wilderness, Jesus returns to the place of his childhood and starts teaching in the synagogue. He walks familiar streets. He eats familiar foods. He surely runs into the familiar faces of neighbors who helped raise him.

The Son of God begins his public ministry by doing what he always does on the Sabbath: he goes to the synagogue. In doing so, Jesus blesses the act of returning. He recognizes the value of drawing strength from the familiar while stepping into the unknown.

With the Spirit of the Lord upon him, Jesus fulfills the words of Sacred Scripture. He becomes who God calls him to be.

Meditation: As we journey through life, there are times when God nudges us to return to a place, a person, or an experience. The act of returning can help us reflect on the passing of time and the ways we have grown over the years.

Return to a place or memory of significance to you. How have you changed since the initial experience? In what ways could you use God's help as you take your next faithful step?

Prayer: God of all times and seasons, strengthen our resolve to live as disciples of Christ in our communities. Grant us wisdom and courage as we move into the future.

Settle In

Readings: 1 John 5:5-13; Luke 5:12-16

Scripture:
[B]ut he would withdraw to deserted places to pray.
(Luke 5:16)

Reflection: *But he would withdraw to deserted places to pray.*

The words take flesh in the early morning quiet of my apartment. I sink into the worn recliner and flip open my Bible.

It's been a long week—and it's only Tuesday. My mind races with thoughts of all that needs to be done. It takes a few extra minutes to settle down.

In time, thin paper crinkles between my searching fingers. Soon their stories sit before me: Jesus, the man with leprosy, the crowds. What will these wisdom figures teach me this morning?

———

Jesus prayed. The Son of God regularly turned to his Father, the One who created all things, for reflection and conversation. Today's Gospel passage is one of several that describe Jesus going off by himself to a deserted place to pray. How did he spend that time? The Gospel accounts don't offer details, but we can imagine.

Jesus likely spent at least a few minutes reciting psalms and other traditional prayers. It is also easy to picture Jesus spending a good chunk of prayer time letting his mind wander: processing the events of the day, connecting insights from the people he served, and simply sitting with God. Jesus quieted external noise so he could pay attention to the internal musings. He listened to his Father—and lived a richer life because of it.

Like Jesus, may we carve out time to escape to deserted places to pray.

Meditation: As we journey through life, God calls us to pray. Our prayer can take many forms including a morning walk, sitting with a passage of Scripture or a poem, or an evening examination of conscience. We can pray for five minutes or an hour. God delights in our time and attention.

Try out *lectio divina*, which means "divine reading" in Latin. This ancient prayer practice is a chance to dialogue with God through the slow, meditative reading of Scripture. Choose a favorite Gospel story or psalm. Read it slowly and prayerfully. What might God be telling you? What do you want to tell God?

Prayer: God of the Word, make your presence known during times of prayer. Guide us into deeper relationship with you.

January 11: Saturday after Epiphany

Jesus Hears Us

Readings: 1 John 5:14-21; John 3:22-30

Scripture:
We have this confidence in him, that if we ask anything according to his will, he hears us. (1 John 5:14)

Reflection: *Jesus hears us.*

In times of agony and moments of defeat, *Jesus hears us.*

When we cry out in pain, *Jesus hears us.*

When no one else seems to understand, *Jesus hears us.*

In times of celebration and moments of triumph,
    Jesus hears us.

When we cry out in joy, *Jesus hears us.*

When we sing out in common songs of praise and thanksgiving, *Jesus hears us.*

Now is the time to trust that nothing can separate us from the abounding love of Jesus, who listens closely and hears us always.

————

Today's first reading starts strong: "We have this confidence in [the Son of God], that if we ask anything according to his will, he hears us." But make no mistake—living confidently in Christ does not guarantee a life of ease. The Son of God knows better than anyone that hard things happen no matter the strength of our faith. Hearts get hurt. Sin and suffering remain strong forces in our world.

To get to the glory of eternal life, we must move through the cross. Suffering and death, hope and resurrection, are always part of the same story. Jesus calls us to move through the crosses of our lives with confidence. Such confidence recognizes human hardship and says: Move forward anyway. Feel troubled and move forward anyway. Feel afraid and move forward anyway. You can do it. You are never alone.

Meditation: As we journey through life, Jesus calls his disciples to live confidently. The Son of God promises presence. Our whole beings—body, mind, and soul—are made to embrace Christ's presence and pour out his love to everyone we meet.

Affirm a family member, friend, or significant other who needs a confidence boost. Be specific. How do you experience God at work in them? In what ways do they bring joy into your life? How have they challenged you to grow in love?

Prayer: Loving God, comfort people who are struggling with their faith. Fill all of us with the hope that comes from witnessing divine love in action.

Brimming with Hope

Readings: Isa 42:1-4, 6-7; Acts 10:34-38; Luke 3:15-16, 21-22 *or, in Year C,* Isa 40:1-5, 9-11; Titus 2:11-14; 3:4-7; Luke 3:15-16, 21-22

Scripture:
"You are my beloved Son; with you I am well pleased." (Luke 3:22)

Reflection: Dear Ellie,

Happy baptism day! So many people came to celebrate your entry into the church this afternoon. We filled the baptistry and looked with wonder as Fr. Nick blessed you with water and anointed you with oil.

Your baptism left me brimming with hope for the church. As your brother and friends splashed around the font, I felt a deep sense of joy. This is church at its finest: energized, excited, together.

I am honored to be your godmother. My prayer today and always is that you may feel God's great love for you.

Love,
Jessie

―――――――

Through the healing waters of baptism, God's Spirit frees us from the powers of sin and death. We join a holy communion of saints and sinners across time who have also been anointed in the name of the Triune God. A great cloud of witnesses surrounds the baptized forevermore.

Ours is a communion that defies death in favor of resurrection; a communion that shrinks the space between heaven and earth; a communion that knows the path of holiness can only be paved by the wood of the cross—and has the splinters to prove it.

Jesus promises that the darkness of the cross leads to the light of the resurrection. On this feast of the Baptism of the Lord, may we draw strength from one another and from the promise made by God's beloved Son.

Meditation: As we journey through life, God gifts us with the Holy Spirit as our guide.

Visit the baptismal font at your parish. Place your hands in the font and swirl the water around. Spend a few moments reflecting: What characteristics does the Spirit embody? Where or in whom are you encountering the Spirit of God? What lessons will you take away from this day, from these sacred seasons?

Prayer: Beloved God, fan the flames of baptismal light within all members of the church. Filled with new life in your Son, help us lead lives that are pleasing to you.

References

December 10: Tuesday of the Second Week of Advent
Belden C. Lane, *The Great Conversation: Nature and the Care of the Soul* (New York: Oxford University Press, 2019), 2.

December 15: Third Sunday of Advent
Richard Sima, "Want to Feel Happier? Try Snacking on Joy," *The Washington Post* (November 17, 2022).

December 17: Tuesday of the Third Week of Advent
Maya Angelou, *Letter to My Daughter* (New York: Random House, 2008).

January 3: Friday before Epiphany
Pierre Teilhard de Chardin, SJ, "Patient Trust," in *Hearts on Fire: Praying with the Jesuits*, ed. Michael Harter, SJ (Chicago: Loyola Press, 1993), 102.

January 5: The Epiphany of the Lord
Benedict of Nursia, in *RB 1980: The Rule of St. Benedict in English*, ed. Timothy Fry, OSB (Collegeville, MN: Liturgical Press, 1981), 19.1.

SEASONAL REFLECTIONS NOW AVAILABLE IN ENGLISH AND SPANISH

LENT/CUARESMA

Not By Bread Alone: Daily Reflections for Lent 2025
Daniel P. Horan

No sólo de pan: Reflexiones diarias para Cuaresma 2025
Daniel P. Horan; translated by Luis Baudry-Simón

EASTER/PASCUA

Rejoice and Be Glad:
Daily Reflections for Easter to Pentecost 2025
Catherine Upchurch

Alégrense y regocíjense:
Reflexiones diarias de Pascua a Pentecostés 2025
Catherine Upchurch; translated by Luis Baudry-Simón

ADVENT/ADVIENTO

Waiting in Joyful Hope:
Daily Reflections for Advent and Christmas 2025–2026
Mary DeTurris Poust

Esperando con alegre esperanza:
Reflexiones diarias para Adviento y Navidad 2025–2026
Mary DeTurris Poust; translated by Luis Baudry-Simón

Standard, large-print, and eBook editions available. Call 800-858-5450 or visit litpress.org for more information and special bulk pricing discounts.

Ediciones estándar, de letra grande y de libro electrónico disponibles. Llame al 800-858-5450 o visite litpress.org para obtener más información y descuentos especiales de precios al por mayor.